Love Is the Greatest

LOVE
IS THE
GREATEST

Messages presented during the morning
devotional hour at the Third International
Laymen's Conference, August 13-18, 1974

by
Audrey J. Williamson

Beacon Hill Press of Kansas City
Kansas City, Missouri

Contents

Foreword

Audrey Williamson's assignment at the Third International Nazarene Laymen's Conference convened at Hollywood-by-the-Sea, Fla., in August of 1974, was to bring the early morning devotional messages. She chose for her theme "Love Is the Greatest" and developed it from the background of 1 Corinthians 13.

It was a most courageous choice of subjects, for most of the 2,000 conferees had read books and articles and heard many sermons on this familiar chapter.

But Mrs. Williamson was equal to the challenge. Her talks were refreshing in originality and memorable in new insights and applications of the New Testament hallmark of Christlikeness—Christian love, the ultimate test of discipleship. There was freshness of thought in every sentence. Her comments were laced with human interest, incisive insight, sometimes disturbing application, and frequently gentle but probing heart searching.

These morning devotional sessions seemed to set the mood and establish the atmosphere for the day. As a result, the conference was characterized by receptivity to the ministry of the Holy Spirit, whose presence was manifest throughout every service.

Perhaps the major appeal of Mrs. Williamson's messages was their practicality, their lack of theorizing and abstractions, and their emphasis on the lasting, the eternal effects of "Christian love in everyday living."

There was no hesitancy about making these messages available to those not privileged to hear them. So here they are in print for many to read and enjoy and receive therefrom immeasurable spiritual inspiration and soul nurture.

—M. A. (BUD) LUNN, *Manager*
Nazarene Publishing House

7

Acknowledgments

I am indebted to many persons and sources for stimulating insights into this chapter, received not only in the months of preparation for this assignment, but across the many years preceding it.

Words have been published which I have read with profit. Ideas have been spoken which I have heard with challenge. Above all, lives have been lived before me which so demonstrated perfect love that I have dared to believe it possible of attainment in this life.

To all of these, I humbly confess my debt, and offer my thanks.

—AUDREY J. WILLIAMSON

1 Corinthians 13

Though I speak with the tongues of men and of angels, and have not love, I am become as sounding brass, or a tinkling cymbal.*

And though I have the gift of prophecy, and understand all mysteries, and all knowledge; and though I have all faith, so that I could remove mountains, and have not love, I am nothing.

And though I bestow all my goods to feed the poor, and though I give my body to be burned, and have not love, it profiteth me nothing.

Love suffereth long, and is kind;
Love envieth not;
Love vaunteth not itself, is not puffed up,
Doth not behave itself unseemly.
Seeketh not her own,
Is not easily provoked,
Thinketh no evil; rejoiceth not in iniquity,
*   but rejoiceth in the truth;*
Beareth all things, believeth all things,
*   hopeth all things, endureth all things.*

Love never faileth: but whether there be

---

*Although the King James Version is used here, the more accurate translation of the Greek word *agape* ("love") is used in place of "charity." There has also been some accommodation of the verse structure.

prophecies, they shall fail; whether there be tongues, they shall cease; whether there be knowledge, it shall vanish away. For we know in part, and we prophesy in part. But when that which is perfect is come, then that which is in part shall be done away.

When I was a child, I spake as a child, I understood as a child, I thought as a child: but when I became a man, I put away childish things.

For now we see through a glass, darkly; but then face to face: now I know in part; but then shall I know even as also I am known.

And now abideth faith, hope, love, these three; but the greatest of these is love.

This Thing Called Love

First Corinthians 13 has been titled the "Hymn of Love," and indeed it is a song, full of sweet word cadences and the rhythmic music of the soul. It is without doubt the most exalted description of love to be found in human language. We have regarded it as a lofty, almost unattainable concept; and while we have read it and memorized it and heard it preached about, to many of us it has remained a beautiful but impractical ideal.

What Does Love Really Mean?

In the Greek language there are different words for *love* which connote different shades of meaning. There is a word for romantic love, and others for the love of a friend, and for love of kindred. The Christian religion introduced the word *agape,* which expresses the divine love described by Paul in our chapter. But the English language is impoverished. We have but the one word *love* for the genuine thing and all its substitutes.

To add to the confusion, in contemporary America the word *love* has become an all too simple, even degenerate term. Love is a patch on the backside of a pair of jeans, a word decorating a paperweight, letters on an emblem strung on a chain around one's neck. It is the message of a daily cartoon, "Love is a little assistance in playing mini-golf"; "Love is tickling his nose with a long piece of grass"; "Love is going swimming with him even if you've just washed your hair." It would seem in the light of 1 Corinthians 13 we need a redefinition of *love*.

We love peanuts and snorkeling and beautiful sunsets. "I love" may mean "I desire," "I want to possess," "I enjoy," "I exploit," or even "I am jealous of." Overindulgence may go by the name of love. So-called love may be mixed with wrong and selfish attitudes—an impulse to coerce, to ridicule, to monopolize, even to destroy.

For all our free talk about love, there is a famine of genuine love in our world. Nothing seems to be failing on such a grand scale as love. We are encountering, not the expression of love, but the frustration of love. We have glibly said that lack of love was the cause of the immorality, the freakishness, the laziness, the loss of motivation, the misunderstanding, the breakdown in communication, the unwillingness to get involved, and a score of other social ills that beset us. And we have let it go at that!

In generalizing we have excused ourselves and let the abstraction dull our sensitivity. We ourselves may meantime be failing to exercise love's qualities and procedures in our own homes—to our mates and our children, in our neighborhoods and our churches. Confronted with our failures, we still hold the solution as given us in God's Word to be an unworkable ideal. We are skeptical about love's efficacy as a practical approach to life's problems. We think it might work in crisis situations but we underestimate its value in everyday living, for we don't have a clear idea of what love really is.

How Do We Get It?

We must recognize at the outset that this kind of love is an *obtainment*. It is the love of God and it must be shed abroad in our hearts by the Holy Spirit. We cannot possibly by our own will or striving demonstrate such love unless it be enthroned in our hearts by God himself. On condition of our repentance and faith, God imparts this love to us.

And then this love must be perfected. We must become wholly monopolized by the love of God. Till then we find remains of unholy tempers, desire for preeminence, roots of bitterness, and unchristlike longings. These muddy the stream of love at its source. Without Christian purity we cannot expect to know much of the depth and power of love.

The highest concept of pure love is displayed at the Cross. There love was poured out upon others without a thought of whether they were worthy to receive it or not. Love proceeds from the nature of the one loving, rather than from any merit in the one loved. When we are transformed by God's love, we see all other persons as objects of God's love and our attitude toward them is one of sacrificial love.

To love and to be loved! These are essential human needs. But love is not a feeling that turns us on or turns us off! It is rather a way of relating to and reacting to other people. This is the love that deliberately chooses its object, and regardless of all else, goes on loving that object. It may be a member of your own family or your field of acquaintances, or the fellowship of the church. But Christlike love is not exclusive. It does not devote itself only to a chosen few. Some have comforted themselves with the defense, "I love my husband or my family or my particular group of friends. This occupies all my time and interest." But love reaches out to the unlovely, the poor, the aged, the rebellious, the wicked, the untrustworthy.

In the vestibule of our church in Leavenworth, Wash., I saw a meaningful poster. Two hands were clasped warmly. One was young, strong, firm, evidently Caucasian. The other was darker, older, knotted, and work-worn. Underneath were these words, "We're different, and sometimes *I* let that difference come between us. May Love draw us together!"

Love Must Be Shared

This is the love that does not think primarily of itself. It is the willingness to give oneself for the sake of another. The will rather than the emotions is involved. Only God can enable us to love like that. We love, because He first loved us.

To love is to be related to other people in such a way as to make them and ourselves more secure, to convey to others that we are "for them," that we are there to support and cooperate with them.

To love means to minister to, to satisfy the needs of other persons, and by this means to relate ourselves to them. The greatest of human needs is for love; to feel that one is wanted, liked, appreciated, valued, and involved with others. This is interdependence.

A tree which stands alone is not likely to do as well as a tree which is in somewhat close proximity to other trees. "Organisms confer survival benefits upon one another." We often feel lonely and anxious, eager to be recognized and accepted. We can escape from our isolation only if we genuinely communicate with another in loving him and evoking in him a reciprocal response.

Christian love is a growing interest in, an appreciation of, and a responsibility for every other person. It is more than a generous impulse. It is a consistent purpose to share meaningful values with another. It invites a loving response, and thus love is increased and shared. Everyone has capacities to love, but they develop only in response to love from others.

Love is a grace and that means it is available to all in the measure in which we appropriate it.

Love Must Be Cultivated

But love is not only an obtainment. It is an *attainment*. It must be cultivated, exercised, developed, and strengthened by constant practice. Everything unlike love in our lives must be recognized and renounced. God intends us to grow in love.

"Falling in love" is an erroneous and misleading term. Love is a development. We climb into love by effort, by stress and strain, slipping back sometimes and starting again. It is a long journey, each person working his way up with others who encourage or discourage him. It is a trial of endurance. It is strenuous, but it is the only way to the heights.

An experience of many years ago has been recalled often as I have prepared this study.

In order to be together one summer, our family spent a month traveling with our husband and father. He had a series of district assemblies in the West and in the interims between these sessions we did some vacationing.

In one of these breaks we were in Utah and stopped in an isolated spot to enjoy the view. Before us was a mountain not too high or rugged and I became obsessed with the desire to climb to the top. There were no clearly defined trails or paths, though obviously it had been climbed before, but not often.

Two unnamed members of our group elected to stay in

the car and sleep. But the boys and Eleanor were game and we started up, each choosing his own path.

It was exciting and I stopped occasionally to breathe deep the crisp, clear air. But as I climbed, the way became more steep and rock-strewn and I began to question my ability to select the most advantageous path. Rough underbrush cut my hands and ankles, and the sun poured down upon my weary back. I felt a little faint. I began to wonder if I would make it.

I pressed on, but stumbled and fell. Then I heard Joe's voice and felt his reassuring arm about me. "Come on, Mother, I'll help you. You can do it. We're nearly there."

John and Eleanor had already scrambled to the top, and with the help of Joe's sure footing and his strong arm, I made it too!

And when we reached the summit and I looked out over that expanse of snow-crowned peaks and lovely valleys stretching out, range upon range to the horizon, such waves of joy and exhilaration flooded my being as I have seldom known. I laughed and cried and shouted until I think my children were a little nonplussed by my erratic behavior.

But in those moments of ecstasy and triumph, the experience took on a deep spiritual significance which has been a true symbol of victory to me ever since. We must climb to reach the heights of love. The cog railroad is not running. The way is steep and arduous. We grow weary and faint. We sometimes doubt our ability to make it. But in the hour of our need, loving hands and hearts will come to give us a lift, and our determination to reach the top will give us stamina. The views we catch as we climb will lure us on and up.

And when we reach the top, the vision splendid will break upon us. Then such overwhelming love will fill our beings that words fail and it will be only "joy unspeakable and full of glory."

Learning to love is no simple matter! But this is the ideal of the Christian family, the Christian fellowship. It was said of the Early Church, "Behold, how they love one another!"

And so, let us examine in detail Paul's analysis of love. I shrink from taking in my clumsy hands this masterpiece of exquisite beauty and glorious truth. And yet for two years I have had an inner persuasion that I must attempt it. I am convinced this passage is not hyperbole. It was not given us to gaze upon and admire like the lofty peak I view now from my study window. We are intended to reach its summit.

Let us put aside the insulations against the demands of this chapter with which we have long protected ourselves. "Let us take off our raincoats in the shower," as Arthur Gordon has graphically said. Let us expose ourselves to the drenching, invigorating, stimulating, cleansing experience of allowing the streams of the love of God to flow over us.

I invite you to take off your raincoat and get wet! I am prepared to be soaked!

It's Love or Nothing

The hymn is divided into three stanzas. In verses 1 to 3 we learn what love is not; in verses 4 to 7 we learn what love is; in verses 8 to 13 we learn what love shall be.

These three divisions have been called,
Love Indispensable
Love Unmistakable
Love Imperishable

They have also been titled,
The Preeminence of Love
The Prerogative of Love
The Permanence of Love

And again,
The Values of Love
The Virtues of Love
The Victories of Love

Take your pick!

Paul begins his Hymn to Love with a series of extravagant contrasts. He describes the most superlative abilities with which one could be endowed and says that without love they don't count. It's love or nothing!

Remember, this is not love toward God we are talking about. It is love for mankind. How can a man love God, whom he has not seen, and love not his brother whom he has seen?

Love is absolutely essential if any area of self-expression in words or deeds is to have meaning. If love is not the motivating force, then all activity becomes mere exhibition. If pride or self-love or money or jealousy or anything except pure love for others pushes us into service, then God looks down and grades us zero. What a sobering thought!

Though I speak with the tongues of men and of angels, and have not love, I am become as sounding brass, or a tinkling cymbal.

First, Paul describes the eminent gift of superlative utterance. Here is one whose eloquence can move the hearers with body-tingling emotion, like a fanfare of trumpets in a marching band can do, or the crash of cymbals in some great symphony.

It is easy enough to be fascinated by eloquent discourse, to be hypnotized by the magic of words. A man may thus impress and influence others. Speech is a marvelous gift. Imagine one who can utter the deepest things of life—move men to laughter or tears, fill them with hope or despair, rouse them to courage or revolt. No matter how skillfully a speaker may put words together, the well-formed phrases, the fine alliterations, the eloquent climaxes, the impeccable diction are of no worth if love does not come through. It is as hollow as the monotonous bonging of the gong in a heathen temple or the tinkling of the cymbal on the drummer's stand in the rock band.

Now the gift of speech is highly prized. The art of communication is the major today for many college and graduate students. But unless we are learning the art of loving as well as the principles of coherence, balance, vividness, climax, and persuasion, we are falling short of the mark.

We may be expert in the techniques that are involved in the many media of communication—television, radio, journalism, the drama, and advertising. But no matter how much we know about the skills of communicating, if love doesn't come through, Paul says it doesn't count.

The power behind our speech is not determined by the extent of our vocabulary, but by the depth of our love. The tongue can do devastating damage, but when love comes into a man's life he has a new medium of expression, for love has a universal language. The current which carries meaning from one life to another is not a flow of words, but a flow of sympathy and concern.

There is a legend about a great bell in an old Chinese city. The royal command had been given that the bell should be forged and that it should be strengthened with iron and beautified with brass, and deepened with gold and sweetened with silver, and that it should be of such size that its tones would sound out over a distance of many miles.

But when the metals were assembled and the work had been carefully completed and the bell cast, it was found that the elements had refused to blend one with the other; the iron would not mingle with the gold, and the silver would not fuse with the brass.

Three times the effort was made to cast the bell but the result was the same. And then it was secretly revealed to the only daughter of the distraught mandarin who had the work in charge that iron and gold would never mingle, brass and silver would never unite until the love-sacrifice of a human soul was fused with the elements. Accordingly, when the furnace fires were again at full heat and the molten metal seethed and bubbled in its huge cauldron, this lovely, selfless girl, prompted by undying love, threw herself into the white-hot flood of metal with the cry, "For thy sake, O my father."

And when, in spite of great grief, the bell was cast, it was found that truly the metals had perfectly blended and the tone was rich and full and sweet and carried out to the distance of many miles. A legend, but timeless truth! There has to be love!

Next, Paul deals with the gifts of the mind or spirit.

And though I have the gift of prophecy and understand
all mysteries, and all knowledge . . . and have not love,
I am nothing.

The mysteries of the universe surpass our understanding. The starry heavens, the secrets of the ocean depths, the riches of earth, the provisions of God for His creatures, we cannot comprehend. Knowledge is accumulating, libraries are full of books, yet the vast stores of information yet undiscovered stagger the mind.

And who can explain the mystery of godliness and the operation of the spiritual forces which affect our lives so profoundly? Yet Paul is saying, if one were so endowed as to understand all the mysteries of life and death and of salvation, this without love would rate absolutely nothing in eternal values. Indeed, knowledge without love repels, for it often becomes bigoted and results in intellectual snobbery. Paul valued knowledge. Ignorance is a hindrance. Tasks are to be accomplished and problems solved. We are to love God with *the mind.* But knowledge without love is nothing.

Lovers of learning are tempted to be so engrossed with study that they do not hear cries of distress. We are reminded of those who said, "Lord, Lord, have we not prophesied in thy name? and in thy name . . . done many wonderful works?" And He replied, "I never knew you: depart from me." They lacked the vital element of love.

They prophesied without love, without awareness of the need of those about them.

> *Though I have all faith, so that I could remove*
> *mountains, and have not love, I am nothing.*

Paul was the exponent of faith; but faith, mighty as it is, is dwarfed by the majesty of love. This thought baffles our comprehension. I look out at Pike's Peak every day and the thought of moving that 14,000-foot mass of granite leaves me confounded until I realize that I had better get busy increasing my love. For if my faith should somehow rise to such miracle-working power as to move a mountain, if I failed in love my faith would be utterly without value.

Men have moved mountains of prejudice and opposition and indifference by faith. But if faith without love removes a mountain from its own path, it sometimes happens that the mountain is set down in a brother's path, injuring or crushing him. Strong convictions and shallow sympathies may result in great, though unpremeditated cruelty. Faith may make a thing possible but only love can make it worthwhile.

The third example in Paul's trilogy of contrasts tells us that love must be sovereign in the will as well as in the emotions and the mind.

> *Though I bestow all my goods to feed the poor . . .*
> *and have not love, it profiteth me nothing.*

Giving all one's goods to feed the poor is charity at the maximum. If it were announced that any member of the church had given his farm, his stocks, his business, his home, to alleviate the desperate plight of this world's poor, what a sensation it would cause, especially if he gave away all of his property and left himself penniless! It scarcely seems imaginable that one could have any other motive for such altruism than pure love for his fellowmen.

Yet Paul suggests it could be so. Philanthropy might have its motivation in an expectation of praise or in a desire to be seen of men. Fear and extortion have provided motivation for such supreme acts of charity. Self-love could push a man to this extreme of self-gratification.

God sees through empty deeds to the empty heart. He balances the books and the giver is left bankrupt, not only in this world's goods, but in heavenly credit. Love does not buy its way.

There follows another extreme illustration,

Though I give my body to be burned,
and have not love, it profiteth me nothing.

Though I saturate my clothing with oil and set fire to it and am burned alive, it will do me no good at all unless love for my fellowman caused me to do it. I might be prompted by a sudden fanatical impulse; I might have a consuming desire to be remembered as very righteous; I might be only very stubborn and this could have been a demonstration of my unreasoning willfulness or even of my pride.

Men in recent years have taken this extreme method of calling attention to themselves. Paul's pronouncement is that, unless it was for love's sweet sake, they have done nothing to raise their score.

The apostle, in thus setting forth love as indispensable, invests life with almost unimaginable virtues and powers. He suggests a mastery of language with heavenly overtones, insight into the mysteries of life and godliness such as no one has ever yet possessed, a faith that knows no impossibilities, a generosity that impoverishes itself, and a voluntary martyrdom consenting to the flames. But one thing is lacking and that is love! Without it, eloquence is meaningless, knowledge is empty, and sacrifice is worthless.

In life's final evaluation, all things shall be judged according to the measure of love that is in them. If we have no love, we have nothing; but if we have love, though we may lack much else, then we have what matters most.

This Is Love

In elegant language and striking figures Paul has convinced us that love is essential. Love must be the motivating and driving force behind any action for it to be effective. Love is the energy which activates us to exemplary living.

Verses 4 through 7 show us how a person animated by love thinks and feels and does. They reveal the beauty of love when it is allowed to completely master a personality.

Love suffereth long, and is kind;
Love envieth not;
Love vaunteth not itself, is not puffed up,
Doth not behave itself unseemly,
Seeketh not her own,
Is not easily provoked,
Thinketh no evil;
Rejoiceth not in iniquity, but rejoiceth
* in the truth;*
Beareth all things, believeth all things,
* hopeth all things, endureth all things.*

We need a refreshing of the love of God. May its

warmth and glow capture our hearts! Love fails when it is superseded by other concerns and objectives that become more important—authority, status, success, money, independence. Or it may be personal charisma, self-assertiveness, ownership, rivalry, privileges, or prejudices. These set up conflict situations.

Now let us see how love can be learned. Love may be difficult to define, but it is not hard to recognize. Instead of attempting a definition of love Paul gives us a description. He shows us how love manifests itself in daily life. He puts love into a world that is impatient, bitter, suspicious, proud—even vindictive. And because love is enthroned in the heart it reacts to these negative situations with a perfect response. These are homely rather than heroic qualities, but to practice patience, kindness, courtesy, humility, and self-restraint requires a more perfect discipline than to do more valiant and showy deeds.

Love can be best learned in the home. The family unit is endangered today. Each member of the household is pursuing his own interests. We must make occasions to let love draw us together again—mothers, dads, sons, daughters. Love is not learned until it is practiced.

The church likewise is the guardian of Christian love. Through worship, instruction, fellowship, service, the church offers opportunities for the exercise of love. Are we using them? Love is not love until it is expressed.

Love suffereth long.

To suffer is to patiently endure wrong. The language forms used here make it clear that the reference is to suffering caused directly by personalities who irritate or injure us, rather than by circumstances. Sometimes this provocation is intentional. The one who thus causes us to suffer may actually feel called of God to chastise us. He may be doing it "for our good." Or he could be evil, "a messenger of Satan to buffet" us, and in anger or spite he may cause us anguish of spirit, even damage to person or property. Sometimes this suffering is prolonged. Love will cause us to endure patiently and without bitterness.

This suffering may be caused, not by the heat of anger or resentment, but by the coldness of indifference or neglect or ingratitude. One can sometimes endure the burn of the fire more courageously than the numbing cold of the deep-freeze. It may not be right or fair, but love endures.

In this matter of suffering long, it helps us to discover, if possible, why it is all happening. What makes this other person difficult or cantankerous, or hard to get along with? Is he overworked, or worried? Is he insecure and fearful? Is he jealous or envious? Is he caught in a bind and is he fighting back? Even so, we look at our children and understand why the sudden outburst, why the sulking or pouting, why the display of rebellion or frustration. And understanding, we can be patient; understanding, we can clear the air and avoid a repetition.

God looks down on His children and understands their petulance, their smallness, even their cruel and thoughtless actions toward others. His overwhelming love in our hearts will cause us, too, to suffer long because we understand.

Having been wronged, love is patient and silent. Unjustly treated, it refuses to give way to wrath. It does not strike back. When it is reviled, it reviles not again. Furthermore,

Love . . . is kind.

Endurance is passive; kindness is active. Love actually returns good for evil! To endure wrong could be just a triumph of obstinacy; to be kind is a triumph of goodwill. Love not only accepts the injury; love is friendly and helpful in return. Love confers good. It does not merely receive the blows; it reaches out the hand to bless and help.

Its first act of kindness is to forgive even before forgiveness is asked. Then love maintains an attitude of forgiveness, not till 7 times, but till 70 times 7, which is permanently. And having forgiven, love forgets and goes a step farther. It forgets that it has forgiven. (Wonder of wonders!)

When our John was just a little fellow, he needed discipline for some unremembered offense, and after I had administered the same, I prayed with him, which he always maintained was more devastating to him than the punishment. He lay on his bed sobbing and sniffling.

Finally, it got to me. I said, "O John, straighten up. It's all over; I've forgiven you and God forgives you, and He says He forgets. So why don't you forget?"

John sat up on the bed, wide-eyed. "Do you mean when God forgives, He forgets?"

"Why, yes!" I assured him. "He says He puts our sins as far as the east is from the west and remembers them no more against us forever."

"Well," was John's studied reply as he climbed off the bed and started back to his play, "I wish you were more like God! You just keep bringin' it up and bringin' it up!" Love forgets! Love is kind!

Kindness makes love tangible. The encouraging word, the timely gift, the compliment are the best ways to retaliate. Perhaps the very ones who are making us suffer are more in need of kindness than we realize. Despondent, mistrustful, insecure people need new life and strength put into them. We must not neglect those nearest to us. Words and acts of kindness strengthen the bonds of love in the home. Cultivation of thoughtfulness for others brings joy to our own hearts.

But we must also learn to show kindness to those who show none to us. "If ye love them which love you, what reward have ye?" Jesus asked. It is here that Christianity triumphs. Its glory is in showing mercy to the unworthy and the ungrateful. Love can conquer resentment. This is the challenge of love.

There is healing, a purging of the spirit in actually showing kindness to the one who has caused us suffering. Do not think that he who thus responds is too weak and passive to do anything else but stand and get clobbered! To suffer long and return kindness requires courage of the highest order.

Are Christlike patience and kindness beyond us? He could do it, but can we? And what about being a hypocrite! "I won't act nice when I don't feel nice!" is often heard.

A man is not a hypocrite when he feels like cuffing the other fellow and smiles and shakes hands with him instead. A woman is not a hypocrite when, after her kids have driven her up the wall, and the checker at the supermarket has made her feel inferior, and the neighbor's dog has rooted up her flowers, she is *still* able to hold her tongue and smile while she gets supper. This only exhibits genuine self-mastery, and the greatest reward comes to the one who lets love do its perfect work within him.

To suffer long and be kind requires discipline. Christian love is not following the line of least resistance. It is a demanding thing. We practice until we become skillful—goaded by a loving, exacting "Coach." When our Joe was a teen-ager, we put up a basketball hoop on the garage. He wanted to make the team. I have stood at the window and by actual count seen him attempt to throw the ball through the hoop 119 times. "Let us not be weary in well doing: for in due season we shall reap, if we faint not" (Gal. 6:9).

"Let patience have her perfect work, that ye may be perfect and entire, wanting nothing" (Jas. 1:4).

Love envieth not.

Envy is pain or resentment at the awareness of an advantage enjoyed by another, coupled with a desire to possess the same advantage for oneself. It reveals itself in the uneasiness, discontent, mortification, which is excited by the sight of another's superiority or success. It usually makes an effort to depreciate the other person, or takes pleasure in seeing him put down.

Milton named envy as one of the seven deadly sins. It is subtle. It enters the system like a disease germ. It must be continually resisted by the antibiotic of love.

Life is full of inequalities. Natural endowments and advantages have not been equally distributed. Comparisons are inescapable. If they are made in any but the spirit of love, they may produce the poison of discontent, jealousy, and finally envy.

We must not only accept others, but we must accept *ourselves* with our own particular endowments, abilities, and talents—or the lack of them. Rather than this undermining our self-esteem it preserves it, and saves us from insecurity. What are we trying to prove anyway? We are all members of the body of Christ.

Parents especially have a deep responsibility to assure each child of his own rightful place in the home, in the school, in the church. To pit the abilities of one against another in the effort to produce a higher level of achievement through sibling rivalry may backfire. Wholesome competition can be stimulating, but when malice is generated, beware.

Envy led to Abel's murder, to the warfare between Esau and Jacob, to Joseph's mistreatment by his brothers, and to the persecution of David by Saul. In school-life envy of another shows itself in charges of favoritism or cheating; in business, by insinuations of dishonesty; in the church, by suspicion and surmise and innuendo. Whenever we find ourselves speaking disparagingly of those who are more successful or more fortunate than ourselves, we should take warning. Even before the words are uttered, if the thoughts of our hearts are ungracious, or if we find pleasure in listening to the unkindly speech of others, we must urgently seek love's help.

Let us rejoice in the success and the achievements of others. If some lurking thought suggests they are less worthy of honor or advancement than ourselves, we are to remember that God is keeping the books. If we get less praise or recognition in one situation than we think we merit, we will get more than we deserve in another. Let's take the average and be happy!

Love does not envy, because it lives to *give* and not to *get*. Love's eyes are upon those who have not, rather than upon those who have. Love is not so much concerned with measuring the abundance of some as with meeting the need of others.

Love knows that in the home and in the church the gain of one is the gain of all. We do not build ourselves by belittling the accomplishments of another or by making continual alibis for our own failure to achieve.

Love may be outstripped, but it does not begrudge others their gifts nor does it harbor resentments. It cheers when a rival wins the prize and the praise. And that implies that it does not retire to its corner to suck its thumb and refuse to participate at all.

In the Bible, envy is classed with murder, fornication, unrighteousness, backbiting, drunkenness, uncleanness, idolatry, hatred. Prov. 27:4 says, "Wrath is cruel, and anger is outrageous; but who is able to stand before envy?" Jas. 3:14-16 says, "If ye have bitter envying and strife in your hearts, glory not, and lie not against the truth. This wisdom descendeth not from above, but is earthly, sensual, devilish. For where envying and strife is, there is confusion and every evil work." What degenerate company envy keeps!

"The Expulsive Power of a New Affection" is the title of a sermon by Thomas Chalmers. And this is the secret. The operating power of love in the heart continually and effectively expels the poison of envy.

Are you thinking how well this fits the other fellow? Have you put on your raincoat in the shower?

Love vaunteth not itself, is not puffed up.

Other translations have it,
"Love is not anxious to impress."
"Love makes no parade."
"Love is not arrogant or conceited."
"Love does not cherish inflated ideas of its own
importance."
"Love does not put on airs."
"It does not show off, or boast or brag."

Boasting is the expression of pride. Everyone recognizes a braggart. He boasts of his exploits, his wisdom, his remarkable achievements.

In his poem "Hiawatha," Longfellow describes Iagoo:

Very boastful was Iagoo.
Never heard he an adventure
But himself had made a greater;
Never any deed of daring
But himself had done a bolder.

This evident kind of vaunting is not so common among us, but the spirit, unlike the spirit of perfect love, manifests itself in more subtle ways.

Now we recognize that self-esteem is basic to human character. To preserve any kind of self-respect we must have a legitimate awareness of ourselves and of our abilities. The world's work would never get done if we didn't. And we must maintain a legitimate concern for our own interests. But self-love militates against love for others if it is allowed to become dominant. If in every situation our first reaction is "Well, what does that do to me?" or "Where do I come in?" or "Where does that get me?" something is wrong.

It should rather be "Will that help others?" "Will this improve the total situation?" "Is it for the common good?"

We may be asked to surrender a classroom, or even a parking space, or to move one row back in the choir. It may be suggested that our office be changed (perish the thought), that we be moved to the annex or to the attic. We may be overlooked when compliments are passed out or disregarded when the public awards are made. One may "vaunt" himself then by a stricken countenance or a hurt silence, and he may be "puffed up" in a cold withdrawal.

Power is a dangerous thing. Even a little authority delegated to us can make us opinionated, overbearing, self-important, dictatorial. All power tempts. To have power of any kind becomes an incipient opportunity to exercise it arrogantly. Hunger for power vies with love.

When our Joe was about 9 or 10 years of age, he and his neighborhood gang formed a "Club" (Capital *C*). They erected a shack of boards and old pieces of carpet in our backyard between my two clotheslines. It was a very private affair. Joe and five or six boys busied themselves here for a number of days, attending to the business of the Club.

One day I found this notation in Joe's room on his desk.

Paul Vancourer, keeps the books
Eddie Mann, calls the roll
Johnnie Erwin, takes the money
Brucie Damrow, sweeps out
Joe Williamson, head boss in charge of everything

No wonder the project soon died! Love *vaunteth not itself.*

Are we really above answering the telephone or working in the kitchen or acting as baby-sitter?

Aesop's fable comes to mind. An ox stepped on a little frog while its mother was away. When she returned she was unable to comprehend that there was anything in all the universe greater than herself. She puffed herself out to her fullest extent and asked, "Was the creature as big as this?" In alarm, one of the surviving children cried, "Cease, Mother, to puff yourself out, for you would sooner burst than successfully imitate the hugeness of that monster."

Who are we then that we should think of ourselves more highly than we ought to think? Love certainly may have its preferences and even express them. But it does not become either belligerent or wounded if it is not allowed these preferences.

Love is humble. Humility does not deny one's own powers or attainments. But it does not boast of them. Learning has its temptations to pride; possession of wealth is to some a temptation to ostentation; people may even be proud of their peculiarities or of their bluntness.

Here again Jesus is our perfect Example. Lord of all, crowned with all the divine attributes, He made the infinite stoop to become the carpenter's son. He "became obedient unto death, even the death of the cross."

His word for us, the word of infinite love, is "Let him that would be great turn servant." If you want to be right at the top, you must serve like a slave!

On that night when He was betrayed, "Jesus knowing

that the Father had given all things into his hands, and that he was come from God, and went to God . . . riseth from supper, and laid aside his garments; and took a towel, and girded himself. After that he poureth water into a basin, and began to wash the disciples' feet, and to wipe them with the towel wherewith he was girded" (John 13:3-5).

This is the emblem of Christlikeness, of self-giving love—*a towel!*

Love looks up into the face of Jesus Christ and down into the face of man and the twofold vision makes love humble.

Doth not behave itself unseemly.

Love is well-mannered. It is not tactless or rude. It is refined, sensitive, gracious, courteous. Love does not do that which is unbecoming. It has a sense of the fitness of things. Love delights to put people at their ease. Love gives insight to others' feelings and desires. It puts itself in the place of another.

Love is aware. Love is observant and thoughtful. Love sees opportunities—to help carry a load, to open a door, to give a smile or a friendly word. Love remembers the one who is lonely or ill. Love is not engrossed with itself.

Love has the power to adjust to every situation. It is flexible. We cannot excuse ourselves at this point on the grounds of temperament. Love enables us to behave courteously, to be guided by consideration for the feelings of others.

Bad manners are usually due to lack of love, rather than to ignorance. The stubborn refusal to "give an inch," or the determination to "get him told," or to "show him a thing or two," offends love's true spirit. Intolerant piety, blundering goodwill, unlovely religion all hurt Christ's witness in the world. Pure love neither gives nor takes offense.

Love is not bound by social proprieties. It may break some rules. It may not be sure which fork to use, or even be sure exactly what to wear, or where to stand, but love is never unbecoming. Love can be trusted to do the right thing.

Love identifies with need. The cry should ever ring in our ears—the cry of those who were shut out: "When saw we thee an hungered, or athirst, or a stranger, or naked or sick, or in prison, and did not minister unto thee?" Jesus gives the answer: "Inasmuch as ye did it not to one of the least of these, ye did it not to me" (Matt. 25:44-45).

Love is like Christ. Wherever He went He was the Incarnation of perfect deportment. In Jerusalem amid the Temple splendor, He was at home, but no more so than on the dusty roads of Judea. He was comfortable with the learned men of the Sanhedrin, but was not embarrassed with the woman at Samaria's well. Lepers and cripples and blind men did not disconcert Him; neither did the elders and the scribes. He was Master when He fed the 5,000 on the mountainside, but He was also Master as He faced His angry accusers in Caiaphas' hall. He was always the same wonderful Example of courtesy and love.

Would we like to always do what is proper and right? Then let us sit at the feet of Jesus and learn of Him.

Love . . . seeketh not her own.

This is the most difficult statement thus far. We are ready to admire the ideally beautiful character who suffers long and is kind, who envies not and vaunts not himself. But now we must accept "Love seeketh not her own."

This cuts directly across all our instinctive drives and training. We naturally stand up for our "rights." We begin to clamor for them before we are 24 hours old, and the habit seems to grow upon us. We are quick to say, "This is my own! It belongs to me. I bought it," or, "I earned it," or, "I inherited it," or, "I deserved it," or, "I won it. It is right for me to have my rights. The law will justify me in doing so."

To maintain their rights, men have split the church, destroyed their homes, shaken an institution, and caused discord in the community. Bitterness, hatred, estrangement, and grievous wounds have resulted.

Love has another way. A man may exercise the higher right of *giving up his rights*. Paul says in this same letter (1 Cor. 10:23-24), "All things are lawful for me, but all things are not expedient. . . . Let no man seek his own, but every man another's wealth [interests]." *The Living Bible* puts it, "It may be perfectly legal, but it may not be best and helpful. Don't think only of yourself. Try to think of the other fellow, too, and what is best for him."

Does our world revolve around ourselves? Are even our prayers filled with self-centered desires or sobbing rehearsals of slights and injuries we have received? The early Christians suffered wrongs and were silent. They prayed for their persecutors; they loved their enemies. And these were the days when the Christian Church made its most phenomenal advances. God give us a new baptism of self-sacrificing love!

The amazing thing is that, when we have defended our rights to the bitter end, often there is only gall and wormwood left. What we thought would taste so sweet has turned bitter. Stanley Jones has said, "If you have your own way, you won't like your own way. Do as you like, and you won't like what you do." True happiness is not in getting and having—only in giving. Love's victory lifts one to the plane of Godlikeness. Shylock in Shakespeare's *Merchant of Venice* demanded the pound of flesh next

Antonio's heart. It was his legal right. Portia reminded him, and reminds us all, that

> *In the course of justice, none of us should see salvation.*
> *We do pray for mercy. And that same prayer*
> *Doth teach us all to render the deeds of mercy.*

Perhaps the most sensitive spot in this whole area lies here. A man may have the strong opinion that a certain course of action is the proper one, the right one. To yield to the opposition even when that represents the majority opinion seems to him to be a sacrifice of a principle, a surrender of a conviction.

Unless God's Word specifically reinforces our opinion, we must recognize that *we could be wrong!* Christian unity has been broken by controversies, dissensions, differences over relatively minor matters. We have solved them by separations. Jesus' prayer was "that they may be one." Love yields.

My father, who lived to be nearly 103, had a profound influence upon my life. At crucial times he seemed divinely led to give me significant guidance. When I was a young woman in my early twenties a discussion had developed at our dinner table about something so inconsequential that I have long since forgotten what it was. But I had defended my position, I am sure, with characteristic vigor and self-assurance. Before he left for work my father said quietly, "Audrey, I have something to say to you. You always have to have your own way, not because it is *your* way, but because it is always the *right* way."

I retreated to my bedroom and cried all afternoon. My sister and my mother came from time to time to comfort me and to tell me Papa had been too hard on me, that it wasn't really so.

But I was crying, not because my father had hurt my feelings. I was brokenhearted because I knew it *was* so. In that long afternoon, I faced up to myself and realized I was developing an intolerance, a lack of understanding love toward anyone who differed with me. All my life that experience has helped me.

We must never deny the right to be right *to anyone but ourselves!* In the home, in the Christian fellowship, there will be differences of opinion, misunderstandings, mistakes, and failures. There will be breakdowns in communication. But love will be ready to adjust.

I heard recently a delightful story concerning Sir Christopher Wren, well-known architect of many of England's most famous churches. He was commissioned at one time to build a guild hall. The building was long and narrow and Wren put in no supporting pillars for the roof.

The board of governors was very unhappy and, though Wren assured them that the roof was stable, they insisted that he add four supporting pillars. This he cheerfully did.

Long after his death the building was torn down. Only then was it discovered that the four "supporting" columns each lacked three inches of reaching to the ceiling!

But everyone had been happy, including Sir Christopher Wren! And the roof had not collapsed!

Love will sacrifice its rights, to preserve peace in one's own heart, in the family, in the church. Paul is saying, "It is good to have our rights. But it may be better to surrender them."

Sadly enough, two people cannot quarrel over a different interpretation of their rights without involving others in the controversy. To defend one's position and justify oneself then becomes a consuming obsession, and in the process irreparable wounds are inflicted. Love's way to solve the difference is completely bypassed.

Jesus said, If anyone desires to come after Me, "let him deny himself, and take up his cross daily, and follow me" (Luke 9:23). Love's way is the way of self-abnegation. Love "seeketh not her own."

> *God harden me against myself,*
> *This coward with pathetic voice*
> *Who craves for place, and ease, and joys:*
>
> *Myself, arch-traitor to myself;*
> *My hollowest friend, my deadliest foe;*
> *My clog whatever road I go.*
>
> *Yet One there is can curb myself,*
> *Can roll the strangling load from me,*
> *Break off the yoke and set me free.*
>
> —CHRISTINA ROSETTI

God, set me free from myself! And this is not made complete in a crisis, remember! We can't let our theories make us numb to the facts! It comes by a process of daily crucifixion. "I die daily," said the apostle.

Love . . . is not . . . provoked.

The King James Version has it "is not *easily* provoked" (italics mine). This has given comfort to many and allowed them to gauge the intensity of their provocation to their own justification. But the word *easily* is not in the original.

There are various translations of this word *provoked:* love is not bad-tempered; love is not irritable or touchy, or fretful; love is not quick to take offense, does not become exasperated; love never has a fit of temper; love is not embittered. Perhaps the best is, Love never loses control.

"He that is slow to anger is better than the mighty; and he that ruleth his spirit than he that taketh a city" (Prov. 16:32).

Surely here Paul is not condemning righteous anger.

"Be ye angry, and sin not" is Paul's word to the Ephesian Christians. Outrage against injustice, cruelty, and so forth, demands our vigorous response. But love remains master of itself. In the oldest translations we find, "Love is not stirred to wrath." In righteous anger there is no element of selfishness. No personal resentment is there. Love is not vindictive. It does not defend itself. It leaves vengeance to God.

Ill temper may reveal itself either in a hasty outburst or in a fit of sulkiness.

Hot-tempered people justify themselves with the thought that the outbreak is soon over. But so is an earthquake or a tornado! Unspeakable havoc can be wrought in a few moments.

But sullenness is equally culpable. The gloom of such dismal protest settles over everyone like a cold, damp fog. My mother used to say, "Now today, let none of us get the 'dumb spirit'!"

We must recognize that some souls are much more prone to provocation than others. How can we learn the art of self-control?

First, we need to determine the area in which we are most apt to feel personal resentment. What upsets us? Do we respond negatively to criticism or to being told what to do? Are we roused by insinuations against our intelligence? Are we swayed by our prejudices? Are we short on patience? We need to become aware of the point of our vulnerability and fortify ourselves against it through prayer and purpose. We must try to understand ourselves.

Next, we must seek to get the other person's point of view, to understand him. Why is he bossy or rude or reactionary? Perhaps he has had a bad day, been mistreated, is sick, or even in sorrow. Perhaps he has information we don't have.

Finally, we need to abandon ourselves completely to

the love of God. His love is inexhaustible and He has abundance to supply our little need.

When a man who possesses perfect love gives way to provocation, he loses the *balance* of his soul. There will come honest differences of opinion which are consistent with perfect love. Rebuke may even be administered in love. Life serves us with small injustices and sometimes with great wrongs. Love can be indignant at the outrage of right and truth, but love is not upset by ill will directed against itself. We must be lofty in our anger.

Love is not provoked. Love does not lose control. Love is a noble warrior.

> *Love . . . thinketh no evil; rejoiceth not in iniquity,*
> *but rejoiceth in the truth.*

Love does not take account of evil. Love does not "store up" the memory of wrongs it has received. The word for *store up* is an accountant's word. The item is entered in a ledger, so that it will not be forgotten.

It is recorded that certain Polynesian peoples have articles suspended from the roofs of their huts as reminders of their hatreds. Christians who keep alive their animosities are in a dangerous condition. I am alarmed when I hear that "hate letters" (some of them anonymous) are received by Christians from fellow Christians. "He that hateth his brother is in darkness" (1 John 2:9). "Whosoever hateth his brother is a murderer" (1 John 3:15). "If a man say, I love God, and hateth his brother, he is a liar" (1 John 4:20).

These are strong condemnations. We need a new baptism of love to handle them.

Love does not cherish its wrongs. It does not preserve them in its memory book. A good memory is evident quite as clearly in the things one is able to forget as in the things he is able to remember. Memory must be brought under discipline. We can select our memories. The way to remember a good deed is to think of it often, to speak of it with appreciation. To forget a bad deed we must refuse to meditate upon it and drive it willfully out of mind.

Love looks for good. Love is gladdened by goodness. Love expects the best. Some people, perhaps because of a chain of circumstances, have developed a suspicious nature. One said, "I never trust a man till he has proved himself." Another said, "I trust every man until I am forced to admit he has disproved himself." A true Christian sees with the eyes of love and finds something in everyone to appreciate and encourage. And how the human personality needs praise!

We make people what we believe them to be. Here lies the great opportunity of parenthood. We need to build up our children in the character qualities we admire. Believe in their possibilities. Jesus called Peter a "rock" when he was "sand."

> *Down in the human heart, crushed by the tempter,*
> *Feelings lie buried that grace can restore.*
> *Touched by a loving heart, wakened by kindness,*
> *Chords that are broken will vibrate once more.*

How unfair it is to ascribe evil or wrong motives to the conduct of another! Here we may make grievous mistakes. "Brethren, if a man be overtaken in a fault, ye which are spiritual, restore such an one in the spirit of meekness; considering thyself, lest thou also be tempted" (Gal. 6:1).

To indulge a suspicious nature can lead to the more vicious wrongs of faultfinding, gossip, and even slander. When love is violated, the Pharisee in us takes over.

The condor bird of the Andes flies five or six miles up in the sky. With telescopic vision he sees the weakened

member of the flock that lags behind or lies down to die.
Like a bullet the condor descends upon his prey, followed
by another and another of his kind. Hoarsely screaming,
they pull and tear the flesh of their victim until gorged.
They become too heavy to fly.

Jesus saw in every human soul, no matter how unlovely or unresponsive he might appear to be, the image of
God in which that soul had been created. One filled with
love will see everyone else in the light of love.

Frances Willard has phrased it beautifully.

> *I pray the prayer of Plato old,*
> *Oh, make me beautiful within,*
> *And may my eyes the good behold*
> *In everything but sin.*

Luther's concept of hell was "a place where people
cheer when others go wrong." There are people who have to
push others down in order to elevate themselves. Their
comfort is "At least I'm not as bad as he!" The real enemies of the Church are those inside the fellowship who
make themselves carriers of pointed remarks, unproved
criticisms, or damaging stories about other members of the
body of Christ. An unknown poet penned these lines:

> *If you are tempted to reveal*
> *A tale someone to you has told*
> *About another, let it pass,*
> *Before you speak, three gates of gold.*
>
> *Three narrow gates: First, is it true?*
> *Then, is it needful? In your mind*
> *Give truthful answer. And the next*
> *Is last and narrowest, is it kind?*
>
> *And if to reach your lips at last*
> *It passes through these gateways three,*

Then you may tell the tale, nor fear
What the result of speech will be.

The Church is not made up of perfect people but of eager, needy people, and of loyal, loving people, sometimes of mistaken, small-minded people. But Jesus calls forth the best in each of us.

Love does not find pleasure in revealing the weaknesses of other people. There are those who, when we point out an admirable quality in another, will always counter with something unlovely or mean. Love does not expose the faults of others. And remember, we can smirch a reputation with a shrug or damage a character with a raised eyebrow.

Prov. 6:13-14 says, in describing such a one, "He winketh with his eyes, he speaketh with his feet, he maketh signs with his fingers; frowardness is in his heart, he desireth evil continually; he soweth discord."

Often stories reflecting upon others are either untrue or are highly exaggerated. Chatting about others is an evidence of an unfurnished mind. There is always a flavor of malice about such a practice, even though no wrong is really intended. Love will show us how unworthy such a pastime is.

Unregenerate human nature takes pleasure in the misfortunes of others. Much of the news of our day is a recounting of iniquity. Plainly there is that in man to which reports of this kind appeal. But love is not like that. Love shares the joy of the truth. It discerns what others did not see of good. To hear the good qualities of others, of their successes and victories, brings joy to the loving heart.

On the tip of Cape Breton Island in Nova Scotia, the old fort at Louisberg is presently being restored. It dates from 1720. In the museum there I saw a piece of china which the excavations had uncovered. It had been broken

45

into more than 50 pieces. But some archaeologist or under-study had painstakingly fitted those pieces together to make a restored whole.

It was quite an accomplishment. No doubt it had taken hours, and perhaps days of careful toil.

I have wondered who is going to take the time and have the patience to find and fit together the broken pieces of broken lives that are all about us.

> *When over the fair frame of friend or foe*
> *The shadow of disgrace shall fall, instead*
> *Of words of blame or proof of so and so,*
> *Let something good be said.*
>
> *Forget not that no fellow being yet*
> *May fall so low, but love may lift its head.*
> *Even the cheek of shame with tears is wet*
> *If something good be said.*
>
> *No generous heart may vainly turn aside*
> *In ways of sympathy; no soul so dead*
> *But may awaken strong and glorified*
> *If something good be said.*
>
> *And so I charge you, by the thorny crown,*
> *And by the cross on which the Saviour bled,*
> *And by your own soul's hope of fair renown,*
> *Let something good be said.*
>
> —J. W. RILEY

Love . . . rejoiceth in the truth.

Truth seeking is the highest calling to which a man may dedicate his life. Truth seekers are peering into the heavens and digging into the earth. They are examining the flowers of the field and hammering away at the rocks of the mountains. They are searching in the books and laboratories and in the marts of trade.

Jesus said, "Ye shall know the truth, and the truth shall make you free" (John 8:32). He declared, "I am . . . the truth" (John 14:6). And again, "When he, the Spirit of truth, is come, he will guide you into all truth" (John 16: 13).

Love is eager for the truth, searches ceaselessly after it, rejoices when it is found, and accepts it gladly. Love takes pleasure in every progress which truth makes in the hearts of men.

"Finally, brethren, whatsoever things are true . . . honest . . . just . . . pure . . . lovely . . . of good report; if there be any virtue, and if there be any praise, think on these things" (Phil. 4:8).

Like love, which never faileth, "the truth of the Lord endureth for ever" (Ps. 117:2).

Love beareth . . . believeth . . . hopeth . . . endureth all things.

Here we have four vital verbs. Love is alive, moving, motivating. Love is strong, dynamic, powerful, active.

Love bears. The meaning here is similar to that in Isaiah's passage (53:4), "He hath borne our griefs." Love gets under the load of life. Love even assumes what is not its own load. It voluntarily takes upon itself the penalty of another's sin and bears its guilt. Thus it becomes the most powerful redemptive force in the world except Calvary. Love picks up another's burden and goes staggering up that hill of pain called Golgotha to the cross itself. This is intercessory love, an atoning sense of responsibility for another.

But love also bears the daily unkindness, ingratitude, ill temper, unreasonableness that are a part of living in this world. Even the best of people have many imperfections and we ourselves have no fewer. So there must be mutual, loving forbearance.

Love is able to face life. It may stoop under the weight of it, its folly and pain and wrong. But it cannot be crushed. It has vast powers of self-recovery. It has elasticity.

"Many waters cannot quench love, neither can the floods drown it" (Song of Sol. 8:7).

Love is capable of tremendous submission. It accepts without protest. Some people discount the evidences of their love to bear, because they are continually reminding us of all the slights and scorns and resentments and oppositions they *are* bearing. Love is strong and silent. It bears without complaint.

Love . . . believeth all things.

This does not mean love is gullible or easily taken in. Love understands us better than we realize. Love looks through the rough exterior, the insolent manners, the ill tempers, the bad habits, searching for something good to believe in. Love is not basically suspicious. Love considers the motive and overlooks poor performance. Jesus believed in the needy men He met. Repeatedly He asked, "Wilt thou be made whole?"

This is not credulity, but trustfulness. Love has faith in humanity. Just as painters and writers take unlikely subjects and bring out unexpected strength and beauty in them, so love finds things that are lovely where most people would not think of looking for them. A famous painter found in the aged, the poor, the afflicted, faces that fitted best between his angel wings.

This kind of love which believes all things sometimes gets a shock and a keen disappointment. Jesus himself chose one who afterward betrayed Him. This is the risk love is willing to take. Love chose impulsive Peter and ruthless Saul, and transformed them into valiant and mighty apostles.

Love sees possibilities. Boundless faith in God leads to limitless faith in men. Love would rather be disappointed in some than to be distrustful of any. Because we believe in those we love, we challenge them to reach up to their best. If we treat men as trustworthy, we help them to be trustworthy. Such a show of confidence often brings an immediate reward.

Our dear daughter said matter-of-factly, when we praised her for successfully accomplishing an undertaking, "Why, I thought you expected me to do it!"

Love . . . hopeth all things.

What faith believes, hope expects and receives. Faith says, "God can." Hope says, "He will."

This quality of hope is vital to all the work of the church. It is the thing that buoys us up. Hope never despairs even of those deeply mired in sin or vice or of those who seem farthest away from God.

Brother Lawrence said, "All things are possible to him who believes; they are less difficult to him who hopes; they are more easy to him who loves."

Hope gives the forward look. It is not blind optimism which fails to take account of reality. But it is a refusal to take failure as final. It is the confidence that expects an ultimate triumph.

Men cannot live without hope. It is love's responsibility to infuse hope into the troubled days in which we live. Because we have Christ we have the answers to life's staggering problems. But not if we lose hope! Hope is the "anchor of the soul, both sure and steadfast, and which entereth into that within the veil" (Heb. 6:19). Hope is more than wishful thinking. Hope's expectation is firmly grounded in God's eternal truth.

Hope sees possibilities in the most unpromising. Teachers, take your opportunity! Let love challenge you with that pupil who has seemed hopeless. Love does not despair. The joy of victory is sweeter when the obstacles are greater. Pray David's prayer: "Let me not be ashamed of my hope" (Ps. 119:116).

On the wall of a homelike eating place in Victoria, B.C., called the Cock Pheasant, I saw a woven wall-hanging. On it were these heartwarming words,

> *Hail, guest, we ask not what thou art.*
> *If friend, we greet thee hand and heart;*
> *If stranger, such no longer be;*
> *If foe, our love shall conquer thee.*

The hope born of love claims the future.

Love . . . endureth all things.

Love gets its second wind. It runs on willpower. It persists when loving is difficult and when the object of that love is unlovable. Christian love is tough; it does not lose heart, does not give up. Love is relentless.

Dr. Raymond Kratzer has a brother-in-law living in Denver, Colo. He is a pigeon fancier. He shipped one of his birds to another pigeon breeder in western Oregon.

Somehow the bird got loose and, following an unexplainable instinct, began the long flight back to the place of her origin. In February, over the Cascades and the high Rockies, through snow and sleet she flew. Unconfused by the thousands of roofs and the myriad of wires which criss-cross the city of Denver, unerringly she made her way to her own backyard!

Love is like that! Love is relentless!

The thought of disappointing the Saviour is intolerable to one who is infused with His love. "Who shall separate us from the love of Christ? shall tribulation, or distress, or persecution, or famine, or nakedness, or peril, or sword? . . . Nay, in all these things we are more than conquerors through him that loved us. For I am persuaded, that neither death, nor life, nor angels, nor principalities, nor powers, nor things present, nor things to come, nor height, nor depth, nor any other creature, shall be able to separate us from the love of God, which is in Christ Jesus our Lord" (Rom. 8:35-39).

Akin to this love is that which binds us to our fellow Christians. Unthinkable it is that we should fail our Lord; but unthinkable, too, that we should disappoint those who have put their confidence in us. Love puts stamina in us. Love is stedfast. This is not resignation, but fortitude. Love is not overwhelmed. Love can take it.

Love does not grow weary. Love is strong. It stoops beneath life's burden and lifts it to the crown of its head and carries it, erect, to ultimate triumph. It bears up, not with mute resignation, but with rejoicing.

For the last 14 years of my dear father's life he was our loving responsibility. For 9 of those years he was blind, and for 6 he was bedfast. Though his mind was keen and his spirit undaunted, caring for him was a confining task. He often would say to me, "Can you take it?" I learned in those days the glad lesson of love that endures.

My husband encouraged me always, and without his support I might have failed. (We need one another!) He returned home from a long, out-of-town assignment one day, came out into the kitchen, and said, "How are you?" "Just fine," I said, and meant it. Then he gave me one of the most memorable compliments I have ever received. "You're great!" he said. "You have steel to endure and rubber to bounce."

Love endures—and with rejoicing.

Love Is the Greatest

We now turn to the third section of Paul's Hymn of Love—what love shall be.

> *Love never faileth: but whether there be prophecies, they shall fail; whether there be tongues, they shall cease; whether there be knowledge, it shall vanish away. For we know in part, and we prophesy in part. But when that which is perfect is come, then that which is in part shall be done away.*
>
> *When I was a child, I spake as a child, I understood as a child, I thought as a child: but when I became a man, I put away childish things.*
>
> *For now we see through a glass, darkly; but then face to face: now I know in part, but then shall I know even as also I am known.*
>
> *And now abideth faith, hope, love, these three; but the greatest of these is love.*

Love never faileth.

"Never" is a long time. Love is of infinite duration and abiding quality. The gifts with which God endows man to bring His kingdom into being upon earth will one day have fulfilled their purpose and will be finished. But love is eternal.

Our concern must be that, in the spiritual activities in which we are engaged, love is dominant. God's love in the heart must be the motivation for all our endeavor. Love is the only dependable, enduring, satisfying way. More than the exercise of any gift, any method, any procedure, love will unite and edify the church and cause its outreach to be effective. Under the control of love, the humblest life becomes a radiant source of strength and harmony. Love is indispensable.

We know in part.

As Paul began the chapter by pointing out that eloquence, knowledge, faith, and even self-denial are nothing without love, in closing he echoes the same thought.

Imperfection, even failure, marks everything in this life except love. We fight against, pray against, complain about a myriad of circumstances. When partial knowledge shall be done away, then we shall see clearly that all things *did* work together in a pattern for good. Here there is never full comprehension. There is always a *beyond.* "But when that which is perfect is come, then that which is in part shall be done away."

Here the inevitable "Why?" rises to our lips. Why accident, why sickness, why disappointment, why bereavement, why poverty and pain? We know only in part.

Even the rich endowments of life remain a mystery. How does memory furnish her treasure house? How does imagination exercise her creative magic? How does reason work, and the will operate? Who can fathom the marvelous mechanisms of sight and hearing and speech? We do not understand ourselves and still less do we understand other people. We misjudge or overestimate. We miss their motives.

And in spite of the revelation of spiritual things to our hearts, our knowledge in this great realm is only partial. Yet even here, in a world which is to pass away, it is given us to lay hold on things eternal, things that will endure.

And our partial knowledge is a pledge of that which is to come. This is the beginning. With all our powers freed from human limitations we shall one day revel in the fullness of life when that which is perfect has come. Eternity will be a continual unfolding of God, whose beauty and glory and majesty are inexhaustible. We shall sing, "Worthy is the Lamb that was slain to receive power, and riches, and wisdom . . . and blessing. . . . Blessing, and honour, and glory, and power, be unto him that sitteth upon the throne" (Rev. 5:12-13).

Paul now uses two figures to illustrate the temporary quality of the spiritual gifts which belong to this life and which represent only partial knowledge: (1) a child's understanding, and (2) a mirror's reflection.

Childhood is a beautiful time of life. As personality and character begin to unfold, how winsome and lovable the child is! We marvel as he grows in knowledge and perception.

But childhood prolonged and development retarded become a tragedy. Maturity must come. The naiveté of early years must be replaced by stalwart adulthood.

When I was a child, I spake as a child, I understood as a child, I thought as a child: but when I became a man, I put away childish things.

For now we see through a glass, darkly; but then face to face: now I know in part; but then shall I know even as also I am known.

Corinth was famous for its mirrors. They were fashioned of highly polished metal. But the image reflected in them was, at best, imperfect and unsatisfactory, dim and vague.

What a contrast with the revelation which shall come when we shall see face-to-face and know as we are known! Here we see only a reflected view of truth as it is in God. Whether we look for Him in the marvelous universe He has created, in history, in the sacred Book of His divine revelation, or even in His Son, Christ Jesus, who is the Truth, still the reach of the soul is unsatisfied and longings unfulfilled arise from the heart. Someday we shall be satisfied when we awake with His likeness.

The partial knowledge of this life shall one day be full and complete. Let us cultivate that love which endures. Only then shall we be ready for the clearer vision and the enlarged prospects of the celestial day.

And let us not make too much of the *now* and the *then*. The now is given us to make ready for the then. Life is one, and there comes to us here a vision of God and a revelation of His love which challenges our capacity to experience and enjoy. We shall be fully occupied if we live this life to the full! God does not wish us to be pining for the hereafter. Even now, we may know the love of Christ, which passes knowledge, that we may be "filled with all the fulness of God."

There is much as we look upward that defies analysis. The mind cannot grasp, but the heart responds to, these sublime truths. One who has been busy talking as he climbs the mountain will be hushed to silence by the view when he has reached the summit.

And now abideth faith, hope, love.

How good to know that there are some things that will not pass away! Note the word "abideth." Many of life's values are temporary. Possessions may be lost, strength may become weakness, the brilliant career may come to an end, the admired leader be forgotten. But faith, hope, and love live on.

We have looked at love as it met the familiar situations of life. We have seen it conquer under every circumstance. And now we are assured that love is immortal; that with its sisters, faith and hope, it shall carry on into the life that is beyond.

We shall not be finished with faith and hope. That they will be expanded and perfected is certain. But they will be, in essence, the same graces we now possess. God will continually be unfolding himself to us, and these vital conditions of our relationship to Him must abide. The unseen vistas of the infinite will always challenge our faith and will quicken our hope.

Faith is the union between ourselves and God. It is belief in God and the acceptance of God as our Deliverer and King. It will finally reach a perfection undreamed of here. We trust Him now, though we cannot see Him. How triumphant will be our faith when we do see Him, face-to-face!

Hope, likewise, will be eternally renewed, seeing more and more of God's glory and more fully realizing the joys of His service.

But love is ever the greatest. Faith and hope are means to an end. Love is the end. For love is God. And "God is love." Love not only outlasts the gifts of time; it also surpasses the graces of eternity. It is superior to the things that perish and it is supreme among the things that abide.

The greatest of these is love.

Paul climaxes his matchless hymn with these eloquent words, *The greatest . . . is love.* He has left the title to the end.

In this world with its demands, its problems, its decisions, its inequalities, love is the greatest. And in the world to come where all will be harmony and peace and gain, love will still be the greatest. The last notes of the hymn die into a silence that touches the unutterable within us. This is Paul's Hymn of Love.

But this gem of literature was not given that we might revel in its imagery only, or only to experience a quickening of the emotion of love within us, or even to feel rebuke for our loveless lives. It is followed immediately with the command—abrupt, forceful, insistent: "Follow after love"!

This is a strenuous word. It implies dedication, persistence, effort.

How can we follow after love? How can we cultivate it? How can we translate it into practical living?

First, *we must be sure that the pure love of God dwells within us.* We cannot reveal love to others unless we possess it ourselves.

Then, *we must dwell in love.* By contemplation of God, by communion with Him, by the enrichment that comes from His Word and from Christian fellowship, we must grow in love. It must infill us, not as a trickling stream, but as a gushing fountain, a well of water springing up within us. We must develop our capacity for love.

"This I pray, that your love may abound yet more and more" (Phil. 1:9).

And finally, *we must be responsible for our love.* It must be translated into deeds and words. We hear, "I cannot bring myself to love so and so, no matter how hard I try!" or, "I cannot help loving so and so!" Nonsense! Our emotions are under the control of our wills. Love is subject to discipline.

Love is not automatic. We must learn to love. We must choose objects for our outgoing love—a mate, a son or daughter, a neighbor, a fellow Christian, someone unknown—and we must work at the job of loving them. Action strengthens love. We must kindle the fire of love upon the hearth of our own hearts. We must not wait until we feel love for someone before we show him the tokens of love—a smile, a compliment, a kind word, a bouquet of flowers, an unexpected pleasure, a bit of our time.

A wonderful friend, a man in his seventies, an exemplary Christian, unwittingly gave me my final illustration. He said, "I and my wife came out of a restaurant one winter evening. It was snowing and sleeting. I put my wife in the car, then took my scraper and brushed and cleaned my windshield.

"It was about to enter my car and drive away when I noticed the car parked next to ours. In it sat a man and woman about our age. His windshield wipers were ineffectually wagging against the encrusted ice on his windshield. He had no scraper and had to wait until the heat of the defroster melted the ice. I took my scraper and carefully cleaned his windshield. He thanked me profusely and drove away, leaving me with a warm, inner glow of love and satisfaction.

"But on another occasion as I was making a cross-country tour, I stopped at a filling station for gas. The attendant was particularly inept. He couldn't even get the nozzle of the hose into the opening in the tank. He wasted gas and spilled it all over the back of my car. I chewed him out [and he has the vocabulary] and for a few minutes I felt pretty good. He had it coming to him.

"But since then I have asked myself this question a good many times, 'If you were inviting these two men to come to church with you on Sunday, which of them do you think would be more inclined to accept your invitation?'"

It has to be love in action! We must cultivate eagerly and prayerfully the love which God has given to us. "Self-acknowledged ideals are imperative," wrote E. S. Brightman.

Let us renew the quest. Perhaps we have never really made it the magnificent obsession of our lives. Perhaps we have demonstrated love only spasmodically or when occasion seemed to demand it. It is the greatest adventure of all, and the most fulfilling; for actually, in the home, in the shop, in the school, in the church, it's love or nothing!

Love is the greatest! Follow after love!